Who in the World Was the ACROBATIC EMPRESS?

The Story of Theodora

by Robin Phillips
Illustrations by Jeff West

Peace Hill Press

Charles City, VA

Books for the Well-Trained Mind

Publisher's Cataloging-in-Publication Data

Phillips, Robin N. 1969–

Who in the world was the acrobatic empress? : the story of Theodora / by Robin Phillips ;
illustrations by Jeff West.
p. : ill., map ; cm. — (Who in the world; 4)
Audience: Ages 5–12.
LCCN 2006901748
ISBN 0-9728603-9-8
Includes bibliographical references and index.

SUMMARY:

Covers the life of Theodora, from her acrobatic
childhood in the Hippodrome to her majestic reign in
the Imperial Palace.

1. Theodora, Empress, consort of Justinian I, Emperor of the East, d. 548 — Juvenile literature.
2. Empresses — Byzantine Empire — Biography — Juvenile literature.
3. Byzantine Empire — History — Justinian I, 527-565 — Juvenile literature.
4. Kings, queens, rulers, etc.

I. West, Jeff.
II. Title.
III. Title: Acrobatic empress.

DF572.5 P455 2006
949.5/013/092   2006901748

© 2006 Peace Hill Press
Cover design by Michael Fretto

**This *Who in the World?* reader complements *The Story of the World, Vol. 2:
The Middle Ages* (ISBN 0-9714129-3-6), also published by Peace Hill Press.**

Peace Hill Press is an independent publisher creating high-quality educational books.
Our award-winning resources—in history, reading, and grammar—are used by parents,
teachers, libraries, and schools that want their students to be passionate about learning.
For more about us, please visit our website, **www.peacehillpress.com**.

Table of Contents

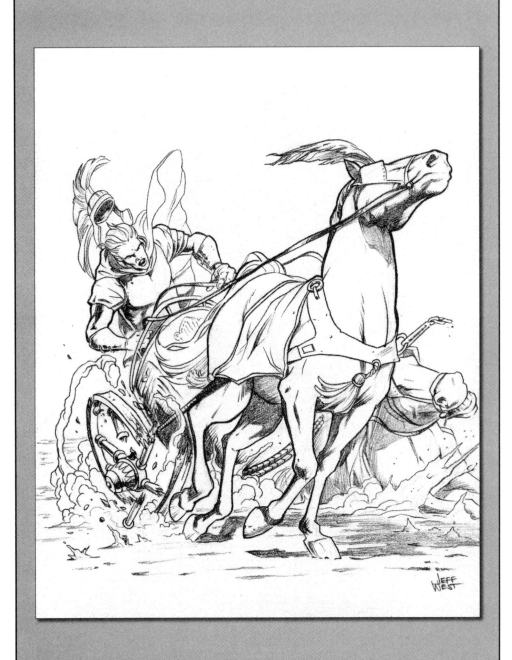

The wooden wheel shattered into small pieces.

Chapter 1

A Plea for Mercy

Shouts erupted from the crowds in Constantinople's huge arena, the Hippodrome. Tens of thousands of spectators filled the oval stadium, intent on the racecourse below them. Two charioteers, one wearing a blue helmet and the other a green helmet, drove their horses around the turn at full gallop, headed for the finish line. A loud crack came from the rear of one of the chariots. The wooden wheel shattered into small pieces. A dust cloud rose from the Hippodrome floor, and out of the cloud raced the blue-helmeted rider. He flashed towards the finish line—the winner.

Slaves carried the green-helmeted charioteer off the course. His sweating horses stumbled as they dragged the broken chariot through an open gate. His fans muttered with anger in the seats above.

Deep inside the Hippodrome, in a dingy corridor looking out toward the racecourse, two young girls listened to the voices of the spectators above them.

"Comita, help me! I can't get my green pin to stay on," pleaded Theodora. Her fingers frantically rubbed the steel of the green pin, trying to thread it through the sleeve of her tunic.

"It's okay, Theodora. Calm down. As long as we follow Mother's instructions and remember the words of the plea, we'll be okay." Theodora's older sister Comita took the pin and fastened it to the shoulder of Theodora's right sleeve.

Theodora and her sister slowly walked to the end of the corridor and looked out toward the thousands of people. The large arena was surrounded on two long sides by rows and rows of seats. People paid money to watch the chariot races and other entertainment taking place below. The two sides of the stadium, and the people who sat on each side, were named for colors. The Blues always sat on one side of the stadium and cheered for the chariot racers in blue, and the Greens cheered from the other side. Now the crowd had become silent, waiting for the next amusement. But the girls had a mission to carry out first. Their father had died not long before.

Now, Comita and Theodora were about to beg the Green fans in the crowd to give their mother their father's old job as bearkeeper. If she could not get work, the little family would be penniless.

Deep inside the Hippodrome, in a dingy corridor looking out toward the racecourse, two young girls listened to the voices of the spectators above them.

"Here we go, Theodora. Don't be nervous. Just follow me carefully, and do what I do." Comita arranged the flowers in Theodora's braided hair and gave her a garland to put around her neck. Both girls walked in to the Hippodrome. They could feel thousands of eyes staring at them. They knew to direct their plea towards one person—Asterius, their father's old boss.

"Do you see him?" Theodora whispered, trying not to move her lips.

"He's right in front of us, there at the center of the stands. Are you ready?"

The girls began together in perfect unison, loudly and slowly:

> Long life to you, Most Christian and gracious
> > Greens
> Life and Victory to you!

The girls' voices sounded small and hollow, and they echoed in the large stadium.

> O gracious Greens, we are oppressed.
> Here we are, daughters of Acacius,
> Who in this very stadium,
> Was a bearkeeper.
> Have mercy.

They continued on with the song their mother had taught them. They knew that their mother had helped their father and would do an excellent job keeping the bears. They thought the Greens would remember this, and help them.

Both girls walked into the Hippodrome. They could feel thousands of eyes staring at them.

When the girls finished their song, they knelt down before Asterius and the crowd. They pulled the garlands from their necks, and laid them on the ground. With her head still bowed, Theodora whispered to her sister, "Do you think they will accept our plea?"

The crowd was strangely silent. When Theodora had practiced this act days before, her mother had said the Greens would begin clapping, and that Asterius would look down kindly on them. But when she looked up at Asterius, Theodora did not see kindness in his face. He was looking up towards the Greens in the stadium, waiting for their reaction. They were not clapping. They were silent—and unfriendly.

After a long miserable moment, Asterius stretched out his right arm and gave a thumbs down. He would not give the job to this woman and her daughters.

Theodora thought quickly, and whispered to her sister, "I know this may not make sense, but follow me." She got to her feet, and reached for the green pin on her right sleeve. With her left hand, she pulled it off and threw it toward Asterius and the Greens in disgust. She turned her back on them, took her older sister by the hand, and walked toward the other side of the stadium—toward the Blues.

"Theodora, what are you doing?" Comita hissed to her sister.

"The Blues will show us mercy, if only because the Greens did not—to make them look cruel!" Theodora whispered back.

"The Greens should have shown us mercy, and the Blues know that. Maybe they will give our mother the job. Maybe they will do what the Greens should have done!"

The girls turned and began again, this time more loudly and boldly:

> *Long life to you, Most Christian and gracious*
> *Blues ...*

The cheers from the Blues' side of the stadium grew louder and louder. The girls continued to sing. Soon, the cheers of the Blues had drowned out the last boos from the Greens on the other side of the stadium.

Theodora and her sister had won their mother the job as bearkeeper for the Blues.

Chapter 2

ACTING IN THE HIPPODROME

Now that Theodora's mother was the bearkeeper, Theodora and her sister helped entertain the crowds too. They turned somersaults and acted out skits between chariot races.

One day, Theodora decided to try something new to make the crowd laugh. She and her sister would pretend to be animals.

When their mother called them out into the Hippodrome, Theodora and Comita got down on all fours and crawled out into the arena. The crowd had just seen the performing bears, so Theodora hung her head down, and let it dangle loosely from her shoulders, just the way bears did. A few laughs came from the crowd as they realized that Theodora and Comita were pretending to be the next bear act. Then Theodora and Comita stood up on their "hind legs," raising their "paws" in the air. The bears roared.

Theodora's mother scowled at the two girls. She turned around and gave the bears a command to roar. Theodora furrowed her brows and roared back. The crowd laughed. They were enjoying this different kind of bear act.

After this, Theodora and Comita came up with other ideas for entertaining the crowds. Theodora learned to mimic other animals. She became particularly good at mimicking ducks and geese. She found she could crane her neck in the same, gawky way that a small bird could.

Pretending to be an animal was hard work! Theodora had to learn all kinds of tricks like walking on her hands. To do her job, she became better and better at gymnastics.

But Theodora knew that she could not go on acting forever. She was getting older, and most people did not think actors were respectable. No one would invite an actor to dinner. There was even a law that said actors could not marry government officials. An actor could only marry another actor!

And that is exactly what Comita did. Comita fell in love with a young man who also acted in the Hippodrome, and married him. But Theodora wanted to marry any man she fell in love with. And she didn't want to spend the rest of her life being despised by others. She had already fallen in love with a government official named Hecebolus. She hoped that he would marry her—even though she knew that it was very unlikely.

Theodora sailed to Apollonia.

Then Hecebolus got a job in the city of Apollonia. It was far away from Constantinople. Perhaps, if she went with him to Apollonia, no one would know that she had been an actor. Maybe he would feel free to marry her!

Chapter 3

SAILING SOUTH

Theodora sailed away from Constantinople, the city she had lived in her whole life, and moved to Apollonia, south across the Mediterranean Sea. She was glad to be in a city where no one knew of her career as an actor.

The governor Hecebolus seemed to love Theodora, and he was glad to have her in his city. He soon learned that Theodora was not only beautiful, but intelligent. She knew what the people of his city needed. She spoke her opinions boldly—even to him, the governor. He often asked her advice on how to rule his people.

Theodora stayed in Apollonia for four years. Hecebolus enjoyed her company and listened to her advice, but Theodora knew he was still embarrassed by her past. She realized that Hecebolus would never marry her. So Theodora decided

She realized that Hecebolus would never marry her.

to leave Apollonia and look for work in Alexandria, a city almost as great as Constantinople.

When she arrived in Alexandria, the local church gave her food and a place to stay. The leader of the church was a wise man named Timothy. Timothy had made a rule that said that anyone who took help from the Christian church would have to go to class twice a day to learn about the beliefs of the church. Theodora went to class faithfully. Soon, Theodora became a Christian.

Theodora made so many friends in Alexandria that she stayed much longer than she planned. She came to love Timothy like a father. But she still missed her mother and her sister back in Constantinople. When she finally decided that it was time to go back home, Timothy gave her enough money to return to Constantinople.

One day Theodora heard soldiers riding by her house.

Chapter 4

A New Life in Constantinople

When she finally arrived in Constantinople, Theodora found her old friends still working as actors. One of them, Macedonia, found her a job and a place to live. Theodora would spin wool and live with Macedonia near one of the imperial palaces. The room was bare, but it had everything Theodora needed.

One afternoon, Macedonia confided to Theodora that she had a special job. She was not simply an actor—she was a spy for the emperor! She spied on the people who asked her to come act at their houses. She used her job to bring important information back to the emperor, Justin.

Theodora became good at spinning wool. She was able to look out her window onto the street while she was spinning. One day Theodora heard soldiers riding by her house. The

Macedonia smiled as she saw Theodora blush.

soldier in the middle of the group was tall and commanding, and Theodora thought he was very handsome. She stopped spinning and leaned out her window so that she could see him better. She watched as he rode with his men. She knew he must be their leader.

Every afternoon at the same time she saw this man lead his soldiers past the house. One day, the men rode by while she and Macedonia were both in the room.

"Who is that man?" Theodora asked.

"He is Emperor Justin's nephew and adopted son," Macedonia told her. "When he came to the city, his name was Peter. But he changed it to the royal-sounding Justinian, after his uncle, the emperor. He will be the next ruler after Emperor Justin."

"Do you know him?" Theodora asked her.

"Of course I do. Why do you want to know?" Macedonia smiled as she saw Theodora blush.

"No reason. It's just that I see him every day, and wanted to know. That's all." Theodora couldn't hide her red face from her friend. Macedonia decided that the next time she was at the palace, bringing information to Emperor Justin, she would invite Justinian to dinner so Theodora could meet him.

Justinian and his men came to dinner the following week. When Macedonia introduced Justinian to Theodora, he was immediately struck by her beauty. During dinner, they talked about the many subjects that interested them both—art and

Justinian and Theodora talked for hours.

law, entertainment and government. Macedonia tended to the rest of the guests, while Justinian and Theodora talked for hours. He realized that this woman had not only beauty, but also intelligence and common sense.

That meeting was the first of many for Theodora and Justinian. As often as he could, Justinian came to visit at the little house near the palace. He loved to hear Theodora talk. Soon, Justinian fell in love with Theodora.

Justinian knew that Theodora had been an actor. He wanted to marry her, but he also knew that it was still illegal for actors to marry government officials. Even though Theodora was no longer an actor, the law would prevent her from becoming his wife. Justinian appealed to Emperor Justin—the uncle who had adopted him. He begged the emperor to change the law.

But Emperor Justin wavered. He enjoyed talking with the beautiful and intelligent Theodora almost as much as Justinian did. She had a sharp mind and a witty tongue. But the problem was Emperor Justin's wife and Justinian's stepmother, Empress Euphemia. She didn't want Justinian to marry Theodora. She wanted him to marry a princess or a noblewoman instead!

Justinian begged his stepmother again and again to change her mind. He couldn't imagine that she would continue to refuse him. But she did. One day as he was arguing his case with her, she turned to him.

She didn't want Justinian to marry Theodora.
She wanted him to marry a princess or a
noblewoman instead!

"Justinian, I want the best for you," she said. "I will continue to forbid you to marry this woman as long as I live. When I am dead, then you may marry Theodora. Until then, please do not ask again." Justinian still loved Theodora, but it seemed he would have to wait to marry her.

Justinian didn't know it, but his beloved mother was already ill. Later that year she died.

Not long after her death, Emperor Justin changed the old Roman law and gave his permission for the couple to marry. They planned a wedding to be held in the Church of Holy Wisdom, Constantinople's greatest church. Theodora was twenty-four years old. Now she would be the next empress of Byzantium.

When the bishop gave the marriage blessing,
Justinian and Theodora were finally
husband and wife.

Chapter 5

A Ring and a Crown

The pointed toes of Theodora's slippers flashed from beneath the gold-embroidered trim of her gown as she walked down the aisle of the church. People jostled each other in the galleries for a glimpse of the bride. Sunlight cut through the air and reflected off the jewels in her hair, the pearls in her collar, and the rubies and emeralds sewn into her gown. When the bishop gave the marriage blessing, Justinian and Theodora were finally husband and wife.

Just two years later, Emperor Justin died. The citizens again crowded into the church to see Justinian and Theodora crowned. Theodora trembled slightly as the bishop placed a gold crown on her head. He laid a purple robe on her shoulders. She, a bearkeeper's daughter and former actor, was now empress of the Byzantine Empire.

*She, a bearkeeper's daughter and former actor,
was now empress of the Byzantine Empire.*

Being an empress was not like being a queen, who could rule a whole country. Usually, empresses were not allowed to govern or have a say in the laws of their country. But Justinian treated Theodora like an equal. Her struggle to survive had taught her how difficult life could be. She knew how important it was that the laws of the empire be fair to everyone—even the poor and unimportant. Justinian respected her advice more than anyone's. He listened to her ideas—and she helped him to rule his empire.

Theodora and Justinian decided to rewrite the laws of the Byzantine Empire. When they were crowned, the empire had many different sets of laws. Some were for the rich people, and some were for the poor. If a poor person committed the same crime as a rich person, he would receive a much harsher punishment. Together, the emperor and empress started to work on one set of laws that would apply to all people, both rich and poor.

Theodora also found another way to help the poor. She remembered that, when she was in Alexandria and had no food or place to live, the church gave her a place to stay. She decided to open convents—places for women to live and work and support themselves—so that women who had no jobs or family would not have to beg in order to survive.

They even went up to the doors of the sacred Church of Holy Wisdom, attacked the guards, and set the church on fire.

Chapter 6

NIKA! NIKA!

For five years, Justinian and Theodora ruled in Constantinople in peace. But one morning, Justinian and Theodora heard shouting from the Hippodrome.

"Justinian, is there a race today?" Theodora asked her husband.

But there was no race. Two men had been arrested for crimes. They were supposed to be punished under Justinian's new laws, but the crowd wanted them released. They threatened to revolt if Justinian did not let the prisoners go.

When this news reached the palace, Emperor Justinian refused to release the men. The citizens' anger exploded into action. The Blues and Greens left the Hippodrome, broke into the prison, killed soldiers, and set many guilty men free. The crowd poured through the streets, looting, setting fires, and destroying granaries and taverns. They even went up to the doors of the sacred Church of Holy Wisdom, attacked the guards, and set the church on fire. Theodora watched the flames from the palace window. It broke her heart to see her precious city consumed by fire and chaos.

The riots continued for six days. Justinian waited, hoping that the mob's anger would pass. But the crowds soon decided that they wanted a new emperor, someone who would do everything they wanted. The mob asked Hypatius, the nephew of a former emperor, to sit in a special seat in the Hippodrome—the seat reserved for the emperor. By sitting in this seat, Hypatius would be claiming Emperor Justinian's title.

Over at the palace, the men of the court were urging Justinian to flee from the city and save himself.

"Justinian, you must go to the ships before the port is burned!" one advisor warned him. "Save yourself, and go now."

"They are burning the city and killing soldiers, and there are too many of them for us to resist," another man insisted. "This is not a small riot—we must flee!"

Some of the men were already edging toward the doors, anxious to leave. Justinian leaned forward in his seat, his hands clenched. He looked towards Theodora, who stood beside him. She alone had not said anything. She was waiting for him to ask for her opinion.

The mob asked Hypatius, the nephew of a former emperor, to sit in a special seat in the Hippodrome—the seat reserved for the emperor.

*"Justinian, you must go to the ships before the
port is burned!" one advisor warned him.
"Save yourself, and go now."*

"Theodora, we may be killed if we don't leave now," he told her.

"We may live, if we go, but you will never be emperor again," she said. "Only bravery will save you now. Only courage will save your throne. You're acting like a prisoner in your own palace!"

Through the windows, the court could hear the chaos of the mob in the Hippodrome. They were shouting *Nika! Nika!* (May you win! May you win!) in unison, over and over. Everyone in the room waited for Justinian's judgment.

Theodora leaned down and said to her husband, "Flee if you like, Justinian. The ships are ready. If we leave now, we could get safely away. But you may wish you had died fighting for your empire, instead of living safely without one. As for me, I would rather die an empress than give up our power and run."

Justinian looked at Theodora. Finally he said, soberly, "Let us attack, and keep our throne."

Chapter 7

THE END OF THE REVOLT

Resolute at last, Justinian sent two of his most trusted generals, Belisarius and Mundus, to gather their loyal soldiers. They had just returned from a war with Persia. Justinian ordered them to attack the rioters in the Hippodrome—all of whom had now committed treason against the empire. The soldiers were tough, seasoned, and unafraid of battle. The savage crowds inside the arena, the ones who had been looting and burning, and who had now placed their hope in a new emperor, were not an organized army. They were a frenzied mass of people, no match for experienced soldiers.

Belisarius and Mundus decided to approach the Hippodrome from different sides and trap the rioters between them. Mundus took his men from the palace toward

When they saw Mundus and his men approaching
from the palace side of the Hippodrome,
the rioters knew Justinian had sent the army to fight.

the nearest entrance of the Hippodrome. Belisarius and his spearmen struggled around the burned buildings and over mounds of rubble to reach the Hippodrome from outside the palace.

The mob in the Hippodrome were still cheering for Hypatius, the man they wanted as their new emperor. Many were still chanting *Nika!* They thought Justinian had already fled the city. But when they saw Mundus and his men approaching from the palace side of the Hippodrome, they knew Justinian had sent the army to fight. They panicked and ran toward the other large entrance of the Hippodrome, thinking they might be able to run away.

But there they found Belisarius and his well-trained army rushing towards them. They were trapped, with the army coming from both directions. After a brief fight, the Nika Revolt was over.

Justinian kept his throne, but the Nika Revolt had wrecked Constantinople. The mob had burned buildings and destroyed stores and homes. The fire-blackened streets were littered with piles of rubble, some still smoldering. Fires had cleared a large area around the Hippodrome. Looters had taken valuables from the homes that hadn't burned to the ground.

Justinian and Theodora began to rebuild their city, beginning with the Church of Holy Wisdom. It was the church in which they had been married and crowned, and they

Theodora and Justinian continued to reign together for the next 16 years.

could not bear to see it destroyed! Justinian and Theodora gave thousands of pounds of silver, gold, and precious stones to decorate the rebuilt church. Colored marble graced the walls and floor. Many-colored mosaics decorated the interior. By the time it was done, the Church of Holy Wisdom had not just been restored—it had become more glorious than ever before. Today this church, the Hagia Sophia, still stands in the old city where Justinian and Theodora ruled.

Theodora and Justinian continued to reign together for the next sixteen years. In a time when women were treated like servants, Theodora rose to rule the most powerful empire in her world. After her, the Byzantine Empire crowned many other empresses—all of whom owed a debt to Empress Theodora.

Bibliography

Angold, Michael. *Byzantium: The Bridge From Antiquity to the Middle Ages.* New York: St. Martin's, 2001.

Cesaretti, Paolo. *Theodora: Empress of Byzantium.* New York: The Vendome Press, 2001.

Dahmus, Joseph. *A History of the Middle Ages.* New York: Barnes & Noble, 1968.

Evans, James Allan. *The Empress Theodora: Partner of Justinian.* Austin: University of Texas Press, 2002.

Herrin, Judith. *Women in Purple: Rulers of Medieval Byzantium.* Princeton: Princeton University Press, 2001.

Procopius. *Anekdota, Internet Medieval Sourcebook*, Paul Halsall, 1996. http://fordham.edu/halsall/basis/procop-anec.html.

———. *History of the Wars, I, xxiv*, translated by H.B. Dewing. New York: Macmillan, 1914.

———. *Justinian Suppresses the Nika Revolt, 532*, Internet Medieval Sourcebook, Paul Halsall, 1996. http://fordham.edu/halsall/source/procop-wars1.html.

Index

(*Italicized* numbers refer to illustrations.)